Teaching Lessons...Defining Moments

Prophetic Prayers of the Proverbs 31 Woman

Belinda E. Oliver

Autograph Page

Autograph this book as a personal investment to a Proverbs 31
Woman that God has put in your path on this life journey.

To Jessica with love!
Belinda   1/20/13

As you read this book
I speak peace, clarity
And understanding into every
situation you encounter!
Love you!

Table of Contents

Acknowledgements

To my sons, Scott Brandon, Joshua Caleb and Josiah Micah; mom is leaving you her legacy and this is just the beginning. Treasure it, hold it close to your heart and guard it with all diligence, for one day you shall see that YOUR life is in His blood and the transfer of gifts I have left for you.

I love you!

Mom

To my mother, Barbara E. Oliver, I love you.

To my father, Walter R. Oliver, Sr. I love you.

To my brother, Walter and my sister-in-law, Rosemarie I love you both. Rosie, I appreciate your feedback and input and for being my sister from another mother.

To my pastor, Judy Moss I appreciate you because it was underneath your tutelage that spiritual components and shifting of seasons in MY life came to fruition.

To my English-Carl, Morton, Poitier and Wilson family, I love each of you dearly. Thank you for loving me unconditionally. I appreciate the support that you have given to me over the years.

To Myra Smith, my daughter from another mother, I love you. This too is part of your legacy, treasure it and grow in the knowledge and grace that God has bestowed upon you. Never forget the spiritual lessons that I taught you, for they will sustain you through ANY storm.

Bryan Thomas aka Mozz (lil bro), Bryan, what can I say? Words can't adequately express nor convey the thank you I speak from my heart to yours. Thank you for standing by and with me during the past few seasons of my growth. Assignments are not always easy and I KNOW that many days you were ready to nail your big sis to the wall, but I am grateful you did not. Instead you supported me. I shall forever be grateful, and I love you.

Elder Sean Ivan Cort, I appreciate you so much. I know we bumped heads and often there were times I could literally hear that deep voice of yours inside my head, "Get to your finish line." Well, my friend, I've gotten to one of the finish lines, for there are always more. Thank you for the spiritual pushes and helping to induce labor pains. I shall always appreciate the love and support you and Debbie have provided. I love you both with an everlasting love, and we have a bond that shall never be broken.

To the crew--Rosalind Colander (Roz), Maureen Stevens (Moe), Steven Randolph (SDR) and Zina Murphy (Zine): I love each of you. Thanks for uplifting a sis' arms during the birthing process. Those loving phone calls, texts and spiritual support spoke volumes into my spirit.

Charlton and Carmelita Daye, I appreciate you both. Carmelita, Charlton's wisdom and feedback have been a tremendous blessing to me and the process of my writing. I honor YOU and give thanks to Him for both of you.

I speak blessings and honor over the woman who has helped give fruition to part of my dream, Eldrina Jones. Drina, I appreciate your artistic spirit. It is you who saw my vision of expressing who I am through "Teaching Lessons...Defining Moments." It is you who continued to speak life in me over the past couple of years. "Power of life and death is in the tongue" as God continually reminds us. Drina, you spoke life to me at a time when I was broken beyond belief. Tears are flowing as I write because the memory of my struggle reminds me that you were always standing beside me, reminding me that "this too soon shall pass," and that this experience would be part of my growth, not just for me, but to speak victory and life to others. I love you.

To my cousin, Elder Sydney N. McKenzie I appreciate you believing in me and sowing into the vision. I shall forever be grateful for your support.

Maria and Anita, who reviewed this book, I appreciate you. Each of you sows into the lives of others on a regular basis. Ladies, we really can change the world!

There are many more people who have touched my life. If YOU are one of them, thank you. I appreciate you and speak blessings and increase into YOUR atmosphere.

His EyeZ

> ## *God's Woman... She Is Her Man's Prized Possession*

I love my man. He is into me not because of the movement of my hips or the swag of my mouth that can sink ships, nor for the softness of my hair or my ability to create his special lair. It's not because of the color of my mocha-latte skin or even the fact that I'm so into him; but he sees me for who I truly am, and for that fact alone I love him. And do you know why he loves me? For I can stand in position, pray and cover him in times of need...when he is weary he can come to me and spiritually feed...and when the tests and trials knock at our door and satan's minions stand in our faces and roar...I will pray that he continues to find our way when life's storms arise but more than all of that...I am his prized possession because...I have God's eyez.

Belinda E. Oliver
September 3, 2010

Introduction

Herein lies a model of prayers for you to pray for and over your husband. Whether you are married or anticipating marriage, this book of prophetic prayers will assist you in getting into position to become the best wife you can be, for it will create an atmosphere of prayer, first and foremost. As women, we often want God to change the man, but these prayers are prayers where God is going to work on you first. I am a living witness and proof of these facts.

Sis, this is what I want YOU to do:

Insert the name of your husband in the blank space and speak with boldness as you pray these prayers. If you are not married, use "My Future Husband."

This book manifested itself prophetically from an assignment that God gave me on September 10, 2010. It wasn't until October 1, 2010, that the Lord dropped it in my spirit that the mandate He had given me was to become a prophetic book of prayers that would allow women an opportunity to pray prophetically over their husbands. In fact when the directive was placed in my spirit, God did not reveal the following, nor did I have an understanding until much later during the assignment that the following things would take place:

1. It was going to take me 31 days--just like there are 31 chapters in Proverbs;

2. The 31 days represented the Proverbs 31 Woman;

3. The prayers would begin to change as I began to write each day;

4. As I wrote in the prophetic, God was creating a book of prayers through my writing; and

5. There would be an overflow in the spirit to allow others to join in and create a prophetic atmosphere in their home.

The day after completing the initial assignment, God gave me instructions to write an additional 30 days to encourage a friend of mine. Further, God revealed that even if there was no response from the other party, I was to write. I responded to God, "How can I write, and what can I say for that amount of days?"

Needless to say, God began to work. I cannot share all of it with you, but I can say that each day God gave me a different subject to write about. In fact, He would often give me the upcoming day's material ahead of schedule. For example, Day 14 might have been given on the seventh day. Not only that, but God allowed me to dream and understand about the day's components in advance, and whatever was given for that particular day was written down waiting for the actual day to manifest.

I had knee surgery near the end of August 2010 and was home recuperating when this assignment occurred. I would get up early in the morning and make sure each letter/prayer was given no later than 8 a.m. Eastern Standard Time. The person I was encouraging was an hour behind me on Central Time, so every morning there was an email waiting for their perusal.

Some days it would take me about an hour to write and edit, so it was no small feat to complete this daily assignment. As with anything we are given by God, we are often hesitant, needing to know and understand if it is authentically HIS voice. I am included in this number, even though I KNOW the voice of God.

Within a week, God confirmed this assignment as only He can! A good friend, Sean Cort, called on September 20, 2010 to pour back into me exactly what I had poured out in writing. God never allows His Word to return unto Him void, and when we ask Him to prove Himself, He follows through every time.

It might not be our timing, but clearly it is His; and this particular time, I needed confirmation ASAP. Sean's prayers accomplished three things:

1. It confirmed my assignment;

2. It helped me to refocus; and

3. It gave me additional clarity.

How can we not serve a God like that? All we give to others out of the purity of our spirit, He returns to us because of His sovereignty and deity.

Another issue of interest was on two particular days in the wee hours of the morning, I was dealing with a spirit of inadequacy. It gripped me like a vice. Have you ever had that feeling? It's as if you have lost all sense of control, even though you KNOW who you are, what you have accomplished and where you need to go to continue the manifestation of your destiny.

God used my friend, Sean, to return some vitality to me by confirming what God had given me. You know how the enemy comes to buffet us in the spirit and sometimes we lose focus of what we've been called to do and what to actually do? I immediately became aware that I must remain consistent and constant, even though I did not have all the answers. This was part of MY JOURNEY to write; God would take care of the rest.

As I continued to write, it hit me that the Spoken Word in the forefront of this book was given September 3, 2010, in the early morning hours. God gave me about one line, which I placed in my email/iPhone. As I sat down later to develop what was given, it took me approximately 20 minutes to write what you have read. I know it has been placed prophetically in YOUR spirit as well for all eternity.

This Spoken Word just flowed from above. As I gazed on the finished product, I was astounded because it was not my typical expression of poetry. Therefore, I KNEW it was given from our Father for it had been downloaded in my spirit, and my fingers rapidly hit the keys as the words flew across the page. I just didn't know at the time that it would be placed in a book--*THIS BOOK*--until weeks later on October 3, 2010.

A Special Prayer

A personal word from, Belinda especially for you, Sis:

My sincere prayer for those who read "Prophetic Prayers" is that YOU will begin to flow in prophetic praying. This model is just the start of YOUR journey. I wholeheartedly believe that upon completion of your 31 days of the enclosed prayers, YOUR prayers will have shifted and changed for the better.

I speak it now into YOUR life! And for those who are truly seeking after God's heart, I transfer into the atmosphere around you the necessary components of what you need to not only survive but thrive and live abundantly through Christ!

If you feel the need to increase your prayers, understand it is the spirit of God dealing with you, and I pray that you flow. What I mean by "flow" is that the words and understanding will begin to connect in the spirit. John 7:38 states that when you "believe on Christ, out of your belly shall flow rivers of living water;" and the verse before that adjures us that if "we are thirsty we should come and drink of Him, i.e. that living water."

Thus, a river that flows is not stopped up and it has the ability to consume anything in its path; and upon consumption it becomes a raging path of destruction. All who are aware of its danger look for safety and stand clear of its path. That is how I see YOU in the spirit--a river that will begin to consume everything around you in love, in gifting, but more importantly in the life that God has created and intended for you to have in Him as He propels YOU TOWARD YOUR DESTINY.

Sis, YOU ARE BECOMING A CONSUMING FIRE! My prayers are with you.

Always in the Master's Service,

Belinda

Remember that "Life is a journey, not a destination…"
Ralph Waldo Emerson

Day 1 - Change

*D*ear Lord, as I lay before You, I ask You to teach me what I need to do to change in regards to what my husband needs from me. I may not always understand the process that You are sending my way in regards to my marriage to_____, but more than anything I want to be in Your divine will, and to do that, I am aware I need to be totally submitted to You.

Lord, our family needs change, and as I share my gifts with my husband (and children) I ask that You release me spiritually to become the woman of God that YOU intended me to be, not my own personal thought process or what others have spoken over me, but the true woman that You designed before the foundations of the world. Please increase my knowledge and transfer wealth of understanding into my spirit for a life-changing substance from above. With that understanding, I can break through the barriers of brokenness and pain and experience the release that can only come from above. Continue to change me so I can be multiplied in You as a true vessel to experience a freedom like never before.

Day 2 – Clarity

*D*ear Lord, as I lay before You, I ask that You give me clarity in every aspect of my life: my faith, my love, my understanding of You and my (upcoming/pending) marriage. The enemy would desire that I not see my way clearly, that I be confused, disorientated and fearful when it comes to my life and my relationships/marriage. Lord, I speak against every design of dysfunction. I speak to and break any fences of destruction by the power and the blood of the Lamb. I affirm that clarity will be a part of my understanding, and it rests in my faith in You God.

Day 3 – Clarity - Generational Curses

*D*ear Lord, as I lay before You, I ask You to show me the areas in my life that are still under the bondage of generational curses. Give me the understanding and show me what behavior is mine (my personality) and what might be laced with traces of those who have come before me (my lineage). Any spirits that have entered my life through generational curses or doors I have opened, I shut each one now in Jesus' name. I bind every wicked force of darkness that comes to hinder my progress and growth in You, and I rebuke the hand of the enemy on my life, my husband's life and the lives of those in my family.

Any generational curses that were spoken inappropriately and wayward curses, I come against those forces now and for the generations that follow me. I come against all sexual, unclean, tormenting, confusing spirits and speak peace and clarity into the atmosphere. Your Word says that "whatever we bind on earth shall be bound in heaven," (Matthew 16:19) and I am standing upon Your Word in Jesus' Name, Amen!

"I will give you the keys of the kingdom of heaven; whatever you bind on earth will be bound in heaven, and whatever you loose on earth will be loosed in heaven."

Day 4 – Love

*D*ear Lord, as I lay before You, I ask You to teach me what I need to do to totally love _____ with unconditional love. Please help me to understand that when I place his needs before mine, I am adhering to the Word to become a proper Ephesians 5 wife. Lord, even when I become selfish by looking at each adverse situation that is affecting our marriage, help me not to see what my husband may not be doing to lead our family effectively. Rather, help me to keep my focus on You. YOU are the epitome of unconditional Love for You sent Your Son to die on the cross for our sins, and in so doing, You became the model of love for me and my family.

Thus Lord, teach me to realize that often I react based on his reaction or lack thereof toward me, our situation and or our family. Lord, I need you to stabilize my mind because I am becoming aware that the enemy attacks my mind giving me wayward and distorted thoughts of what love consists of, but he doesn't reveal that love is constant and comes from above first. Lord, teach me strategies to keep the home fires burning between my husband and me.

As I become more pliable in Your presence, I am becoming aware that often my insecurities are part of past pain and the consequences that was placed upon women from the fall of mankind. Lord, YOU said my desire is toward my husband, thus Lord teach me that love and submission go hand-in-hand, creating a peaceable atmosphere, and Lord, when he (my husband) will not do right by me, Lord I promise to leave him in YOUR hands for appropriate measures of sustainability surrounding our marriage and love.

Day 5 – Honesty and Transparency

Dear Lord, as I lay before You, I ask You to teach me about honesty and transparency with my husband. Lord, I realize it is with You first that I must bare my soul to understand that I only become worthy through and by Your blood that was shed on the cross; that I must first come to You to receive understanding of even how to live a life of transparency.

Lord, continue to keep my cup overflowing with YOUR love that I might give to others. Continue to teach me who YOU are during my personal encounters with You because You are my example of UNCONDITIONAL love; and that love permits me to forgive others as You have forgiven me. Thus, Lord, my prayer is for continued honesty and transparency in all that is forthcoming in my life.

Lord, give me increased intimacy with You, so You can keep my cup running full, so there is an undeniable overflow of Your spirit and a recourse of expeditious ability to give to others in regards to being honest and transparent.

Day 6 - Pastor-ship

*D*ear Lord, as I lay before You, I ask You to teach me what I need to do to be the kind of wife that supports her husband as he ministers to others. The ability to motivate and inspire others is a true gift and not of our own abilities, but it resides and comes from above.

Lord, I ask that as my husband continues to pour out to others, that You will fill him back up; and more so teach me how to love him throughout the entire process as You, he and I create a three-fold cord in our marriage.

Day 7 - Prophetic Mantle

*D*ear Lord, as I lay before You, I ask You to teach me what I need to do to be cognizant of Your divine will in my life and the life of my husband. Lord there are many who believe that prophetic gifts are not from You and many who do believe; while there are others who believe they should be used for their own accord. But today, Lord I ask that You teach me how to stand before You, that I might understand that prophecy truly is for the propagation of experiencing the mighty and glorious power of YOU!

Lord, if I lack faith in this area, I ask for increase. If I do not understand, I ask for understanding. Lord, teach me to remain humble before You as You send increase in this area into my life, and into the life of my husband and those to whom I am connected.

Day 8 - Fear of Rejection

*D*ear Lord, as I lay before You, I ask You to teach me what I need to be, and how to be aware of the fear of rejection in my life, that of my husband and those to whom I am connected. No one likes rejection, but teach me to understand that often the enemy uses rejection as a weapon to keep wives from truly loving their husbands; and for husbands to withhold from their wives.

Lord, Your Word tells us "perfect love casts out all fear," so it is with this understanding that I willingly submit to the leadership of my husband. Teach him all he needs to know to understand me and treat me accordingly. Lord, I bind all forces that are associated with or have attached themselves to our life in regards to the fear of rejection. This applies to past, generational and any future components as you propel me forth through my various seasons of life as well as any assignments that You lay at my feet.

Lord, I speak to each spirit directly, whether it be one or many, because Jesus Christ's submission on the cross allows me freedom of experience like no other. Anything attempting to thwart the work of God in my life, that of my husband and those

I am connected to, I demand that it must stand down as God moves me into the call He has for MY life. I bind the spirits of torment in this area and speak peace to MY mind and spirit. Lord, I thank You for deliverance in every area. In Jesus' name, amen and amen, and as the prayer stated previously, it is so!

Day 9 – Anger

*D*ear Lord, as I lay before You, I ask You to teach me what I need to know about anger in my own life. Often, anger is a response to my disappointment; hence my reactions may not always be appropriate or Godly. So Lord, I ask for Your assistance by teaching me discipline, balance and teaching me not to allow the enemy entry into my life through my anger.

In addition, Lord, I need Your help when my husband expresses anger because I need to understand that his reactions might need to be charged to his head and not his heart. This exponent often ties in to the fear of rejection, so Lord, I bind all inappropriate spirits in both our lives as we continue to learn to walk as one. More importantly, Lord, teach me discipline, because controlling my anger is vital to my growth and the growth of my husband, my family and those to whom I am connected.

Lord, give me balance as you send the abundance of prophetic rain. Lord, I want YOU to reign in my life and I submit every inappropriate fiber of my being to You as You teach me to submit my anger unto You.

Day 10 - Humble Servant

*D*ear Lord, as I lay before You, I ask You to teach me to be a woman of humility for true power lies in the discipline of humility and not in one's ego. Lord, my husband's ego and mine cannot compete with each other; therefore, I thank You for my ability to submit to him and Your process for our lives.

Lord, I am Your humble servant. I place all self-interest, self-awareness and self-thought processes at Your feet to be mastered appropriately. Lord, when others come to thwart my purpose and the design of my life that You spoke into existence even before my birth; I declare that their plans are aborted and laid at Your throne, and their exposure and attacks in my life will become apparent to be seen by all. More so, I place the seed of forgiveness in my heart now because attacks are from satan to buffet my growth. Lord, I receive my growth with humility and thankfulness in each season, because it has been designed by You to foster my maturity in regards to becoming and being a humble servant.

Day 11 - Fear of Inadequacy

*D*ear Lord, as I lay before You, I ask You to teach me how to combat the feelings of inadequacy that the enemy tries to send my way. I make this request with an awareness that life's battles have a way of tiring my spirit, and those are the times when I feel the most inadequate. However, Lord, You have told me through Your Word that I am more than a conqueror, which means not only can I conquer my fears, but I can stand when the forces of hell rise up against me.

Lord, I thank You for complete balance in my life, mind and spirit. I rebuke every feeling and spirit of inadequacy in my life and in the atmosphere surrounding me, in Jesus' name, amen!

Day 12 - Spiritual Mother

Prayer Number 1

Dear Lord, as I lay before You, I ask You to teach me how to become a "true" spiritual mother. Mothers have a heart for children, whether they have a child or not. Help me to understand that giving birth is not always from my physical womb, but also encompasses spiritual birth. To do that, I must be in spiritual position and relationship with You first.

Lord, I need to know and hear Your heart, that I might give to those around me. I want to be able to minister to someone and have the ability to see beyond what my natural eyes can ascertain. Lord, I need Your eyes to see through all situations.

Day 12 - Spiritual Mother

Prayer Number 2

*D*ear Lord, as I lay before You, I ask You to teach me how to become a spiritual mother to those who are downtrodden and less fortunate. Help me to become one who has a willing ear to hear problems and to assist by coming up with supernatural solutions that can only come from Your divine guidance.

There are many people in the world who need help outside my family and inner circle, and Lord, I know You tell us to bless others. Thus, I want that to become a natural part of me--to easily lend a hand when needed. Teach me to understand that as I give to others, You will always restore back to me in the spirit with which I poured out.

Day 13 – Submission

*D*ear Lord, as I lay before You, I ask You to teach me how to become truly submitted according to YOUR Will that You have for my life. It is because of lack of understanding that many do not realize that true submission is powerful when it is activated properly in our lives.

Lord, help me to be aware when the enemy opens the door for manipulation to take place, because, Lord, I want to have a level of clarity surrounding this area and I want to KNOW the difference between submission and manipulation. Lord, I want everything that You have for me and my family according to Your Word. In order to attain this, I realize I must submit my will to You first and then to my husband.

God, I truly want what's best for me, and I ask that You teach me to humbly lay down my thought process in genuine submission, so I might be free to live abundantly in all areas of my life. Lord, this is my sincere prayer of truth and clarity, and I speak freedom in MY OWN life in regards to submission, in Jesus' name, amen!

Day 14 - Innovative Ideas

*D*ear Lord, as I lay before You, I ask You to teach me how to become an innovator of Your Word and will for my life and that of my family. The world has a system, but mankind can only see so far into the future. You are a God that sees and knows all. I incorporate Your ideas into my spiritual repertoire, that my spirit might be creative, innovative and so inviting that it would minister to the needs of my family and others around me.

I speak creativity and innovative ideas into my spirit today. As I continue my walk with You, I ask that You download those necessary components into my spirit with grace, freedom and abundance. Lord I willingly affirm and attest to the fact that I am a walking incubator of innovativeness for YOUR Kingdom.

Day 15 – Consistency

*D*ear Lord, as I lay before You, I ask You to teach me how to become a woman of consistency in every area of my life--consistency in actions, deeds and words in regards to my life and ministry. Your Word tells us it is the "little foxes that destroy the vine," and so often it is the little things that distract me from handling the spiritual directives that You continually speak into my life.

Lord, as I pray this particular prayer today, I speak consistency into my life and speak clarity surrounding this spiritual component; and that any area that might have a small tear (in the spirit) through neglect or disregard or even any small unnoticed thing, that God Almighty, YOU seal it up now in the spirit.

I speak against any satan-driven agendas from people that I or my husband might be connected to; Lord, keep us covered, even so right now. Father, allow consistency to course through the very fibers of my being and lodge itself in my spirit, that no force can withstand the power of it, for it has been placed there by YOU.

Lord, I declare that the same be applied to those who I am rightfully connected to and to those that YOU connect me to, in Jesus' name I pray, amen!

Day 16 – Adaptability

*D*ear Lord, as I lay before You, I ask You to teach me how to become a woman who easily adapts to the situations around her. Often, life brings us many changes, and when we cannot adjust our lives based on what You said, the enemy comes in like a flood to destroy the things that You have given to us. Thus, Lord we pull down the strongholds of torment, fear and rigidness and ask for increased faith.

Lord, as You have been dealing with me, I am realizing that I must be able to adjust, adapt, grow and succeed on many levels when I am in a loving relationship with my husband and those to whom I am connected. There are those who regard adaptability as a system, a process of change, even a discipline. Lord, I can NOW see that discipline is needed for Your Kingdom. I am also aware that in dealing with my husband and those I am connected to, I must have an attitude of "going with the flow;" yet I must also be able to distinguish the difference between defining a proper relationship that exudes and executes love; but more so I must gain an understanding of how YOU would proceed in applying love properly to the situation at hand.

I know You are not a God of nor the author of confusion, but I also know that many times satan rears his head to cause havoc and chaos in my life. So, today I stand in position to request assistance for the future and what is to come. I address these areas now with the understanding that as the foundation is laid You will teach me to adjust and adapt, create a discipline, a sequence of moving forward of continual motions that keep me propelling in the area of spiritual forces--for YOUR Glory. I speak these things into the atmosphere now.

Teach me entirely what YOU want me to know about adaptability. Show me Your face in regards to this area. Give me YOUR eyes. Increase my knowledge and strength and understanding in this area, and as I continue to seek YOUR face, bless me and my husband and those I am connected to with strategic wisdom that can only come from You. Any forces that come to bind, hinder and keep us or hold us in this area, we rebuke in Jesus' name, amen, for it has been declared and so shall it be!

Day 17 - Fear of Isolation

*D*ear Lord, as I lay before You, I ask You to teach me to combat the tactics of the enemy in regards to feelings of isolation. Any concerns from my past childhood, adolescence or even recent events that have brought about fear of being isolated by others, I bind in the precious name of Jesus. I rebuke every wayward spirit of fear and isolation that the enemy has sent my way and speak clarity and freedom to each corner and situation in my life because, Lord, YOU know all things-- from the moment of my conception until the moment that You request me to leave this earth.

You know my down-sitting and my uprising; You know the very amount of hairs that are recorded on my head. You know what I love and who I love and what I fear. Lord, You are my sustainer above all else. Today, I lay my all on the altar and ask that You purge me in the appropriate areas for it is my intense desire to serve You and Your people. No matter what my fleshy desire might be, I want nothing to come between me and what You have for me to accomplish. I am aware that to release all that You have laid at my doorstep, I must remain humble, pliable and stay in a zone of submission to accomplish the greatness that is before me, my husband and those to whom I am connected.

Therefore, God, I ask that You keep me on the straight and narrow as the path is laid out, and as things began to unfold according to YOUR plan and will, make all things plain and give us YOUR eyes in every situation. I ask for the understanding surrounding the fear of isolation as it begins to unfold, for it is with understanding that this has been given today, whether for me or for my husband or for the people that have been placed in our path of ministry.

Lord, assist in slicing through the stigma of this spirit and give clarity surrounding this particular force. All that we do is for YOUR glory and for YOUR Kingdom. For those who seek to destroy, I ask You send Your warriors of ministry and put them in place now for that appropriate time. Send Your spirit of peace and love to assist in accomplishing all that You set forth before the foundations of the world. I thank You for this and for increased knowledge, wisdom, clarity and understanding, in Jesus' name I pray, amen!

Day 18 – Reliability

*D*ear Lord, as I lay before You, I ask You to teach me to be constant in the lives of those who depend and rely on me. A woman has the ability to wear many hats, such as mother, wife, sister, friend, lover, and teacher, in the lives of those she reaches. These responsibilities can weary a woman's spirit, because many pull upon who she is to them.

I ask that You teach me how to recharge my spirit in You. More importantly, give me the ability to assess how the people in my life need me, and make me accountable to You first, Lord, for I have turned my life over to You for YOUR glory. Thus, Lord, give me an understanding that whenever we grow within the spiritual components You place in our life that changes and shifts within the spirit occurs. Lord, I ask that You cover me in this area.

All I do is for YOUR glory and the building up of YOUR Kingdom. Sometimes, I might not be aware of where I lack in certain areas, but You told me that anything that I ask for in Your name, believing, I shall receive. You also told me that You wouldn't withhold good things from me and, Lord, I confess that sometimes I am not worthy of You nor Your grace, but I stand in faith of expectation.

Make me more aware in this particular area, and at the same time, keep me, my husband and those I am connected to covered, and send increased knowledge and wisdom that only comes from You. I bind the forces of inconsistency, confusion and strife that come to abort the very plan of God.

I thank You because as others rely on me, I, in turn, will teach the same things that You gave me to them. I ask for increased peace in every area of my life, and bind the spirits of torment. Lord, I thank You for showing me Your face and favor, in Jesus' name, I pray, amen!

Day 19 – Steadfastness

Dear Lord, as I lay before You, I ask You to teach me steadfastness in regards to my relationship with You first, for if I cannot be stable in my relationship with You, I cannot be accountable in my spiritual walk with others. Lord I need to understand that my flesh houses my spirit and that whichever one I feed, it will become the stronger, thus stability is vital to my walk with You.

I need to know "who I am" in my flesh so I can understand "who I belong to in the spirit." Lord, sharpen my eyes, so I can be focused and stable. I request an increase of knowledge from above to understand my humanity, my strengths and my weakness, but more importantly, I request You teach me to be a stable warrior in You! Lord, because of my knowledge and love for You, I am willing to sacrifice "who I am" in my flesh to remain "whose I am" in my spirit.

Lord, as I seek You for understanding in regards to maintaining position in the upcoming seasons of my life, I ask that as the seasons shift and whatever task is at hand, that You would steady me. I also ask You to cover me from the top of my head to the soles of my feet.

Lord, maintain the vision You have given me. I speak clarity into the atmosphere to reveal any spiritual exposure that is not from You. Sharpen my eyes, help me to be focused and stable and send increase in knowledge and wisdom to not only understand me and my humanity but to also be an incubator of knowledge that I might give to others in this very area. God, I need YOU as things began to unfold, for position in Your Kingdom is important and will be evident, but the position is not for notoriety but for service unto YOU.

I thank You for positions of stability. Teach me not to move to the right or the left, until You release me. Teach me to stand in position with peace in my mind and spirit. I bind any spirits of confusion, strife, and torment in this particular area, and declare that the glory of God will unfold to be manifest according to Your will. In Jesus' name we pray, amen!

Day 20 – Character

*D*ear Lord, as I lay before You, I ask You to teach me about the validity of one's character. Lord, it doesn't matter whether my parents and/or extended family gave me the proper instruction concerning the building up of one's character; for now I've approached You as my Lord and Savior, and I am boldly coming before Your throne for YOU to give me instruction in this particular area.

Lord, You said "I am more than a conqueror," thus I need You to teach me how to stand against the advances of the enemy who comes to sift me as wheat and destroy me when I make a stand to do right in Your eyes. Lord, teach me to rest upon Your power that resides inside of me. Lord, I want to be an example before my husband, my children, my family and my community. Lord, I want to be known as a woman of character and integrity who chooses to do the right and necessary things of my Father, my King and my earthly King (my husband), for Lord it is never about my past, but ALWAYS about my future, for Lord I am a work in progress.

Lord, only You know what I have to accomplish in You; thus Lord I ask that You set me aside for the wonderful and mighty works of Your Kingdom. Lord, continue to give me additional clarity in this particular area and I speak today to any spiritual components that are not of You Father, because I realize the enemy comes to steal, kill and destroy. It is his desire that I NEVER accomplish my destiny. It is his desire to show the world that a woman of God cannot stand in the face of adversity and denounce his wicked works. Yet I stand because I know that Christ came to conquer and gave ME the ability to be a conqueror when I stand on the Word and stand in faith of the power that resides within me.

Lord, You give me power when I use the internal power of the Holy Ghost--that good shifting of my tongues (speaking in tongues) that can bring forth destruction in satan's kingdom. The power of life and death resides within me (my tongue), Lord, and I can speak life to those who have only seen despair and destruction. Lord, I thank You for this as You continue to make me an example. Lord, I cover any exposed areas in my life as You begin to expand and expound them before my eyes, and as they are revealed I immediately cover them in prayer and by the blood that was shed on the cross.

You came to make me victorious in YOU. You promised that anything I ask in Your name, believing, I shall receive and I stand in expectation of the abundance of the outpouring of Your blessings and the building up in the area of character and integrity. I speak the words now, that no matter how powerful the spirit/enemy that comes to attack, I stand NOW--TODAY-- and pull down that stronghold in the spirit.

I also speak to any future attack(s) and withstand against it TODAY and from THIS point forward. Lord, I have no time for foolishness, for the time has been shortened, and there is an abundance of Kingdom work that needs to be accomplished. Satan, you are a liar and no truth resides in you, and I declare today that I am a woman of impeccable character and integrity, from the top of my head to the soles of my feet. I declare this in Jesus' name I pray, amen and amen, and God said it is so!

Day 21 – Commitment

*D*ear Lord, as I lay before You, I ask You to teach me about commitment, because I live in a world that often portrays a lack of commitment in regards to relationships, friendships and love overall. Yet God, I know that if You resonate commitment in my spirit, it will begin to change the atmosphere around me, for I need to be able to discern the difference between levels of commitment to You first and then to others as I encounter them.

Help me to count up the costs of my relationships, so that I understand that when I commit, it is based on unconditional love. On the other side of the coin, help me to be aware that I might have to create boundaries to keep myself covered from those who seek to destroy me. Therefore, Lord, teach me balance in all areas. As the seasons in my life change, based upon my growth, I request that You keep me humble in this area as I commit my thought process and mindset to YOU, so YOU can rearrange it according to YOUR mind.

Allow me to fulfill YOUR plan(s) in my life and in the lives of my husband and my family and those to whom I am connected. I request that You allow me to discern the people who will come to shatter and shake the very essence of what You have declared surrounding commitment in MY life, and we stop them at the door in the spirit. Lord, my commitment is first to YOU and to fulfilling the promises You have declared over me to build Your Kingdom.

Lord, allow that commitment to tie me to You, so that You can showcase me as YOUR property. Lord, I understand that many have started out, but didn't count up the cost and they fell by the wayside; but this scenario will not occur in my life, for I speak to every spiritual situation and or problem that will try to circumvent the plan of God. I bind the wicked forces now and for all times.

God, You gave me time, and it is with realization that I will make the best use of that time. Lord, I declare that no wedge driven by outside forces will succeed, and I will stand in a spirit of solidarity with You as the area of commitment in my life will be a force to be reckoned with, as You move the vision for my life forward.

Day 22 - Passion for Life

*D*ear Lord, as I lay before You, I ask you to teach me about living and loving passionately according to YOUR will. Lord You are my sustainer and the giver of life, and often the tests and trials that come my way tear at my spirit and keep me on a perpetual cycle of heaviness, which is often attributed to warfare with the enemy.

Lord, help me to discern these situations and realize that I am at war, but the enemy is not my spouse or my husband to be, it is satan himself. It is his desire to keep me off balance and unfocused because he knows that anything I do for You passionately has an effect in the atmosphere; and affects others as I become Your catalyst for change. Lord, YOU are my sustainer, and when it feels like my energy and stamina is low I will remember to look unto the hills for my help is nigh. Help me to be cognizant that I exist because of YOUR Passion for MY Life, and that YOU gave up YOUR life so I might continue to live passionately.

Lord, I ask that You give me a portion of your passion and allow it to course through my veins that I can continue to fight the battles for my husband, my family and those to whom I am connected. Help me to keep my mind stayed on You, as You continue to release peace into my atmosphere and a level of clarity that surpasses every situation that is convoluted with demonic activity.

Lord, I will lean upon YOU in my storms and allow You to be the helmsman as I humbly submit to You as You chart the course for my life. Lord, I will be passionate for YOU, the lover of my soul.

Day 23 – Opposition

*D*ear Lord, as I lay before You, I ask You to teach me about the spirit of opposition in my life, my husband's and the lives of those to whom I am connected. Lord, if I am the opposing force, then show me myself and my weak areas regarding my own growth.

Lord, I understand that anytime I become more connected to You, opposition will come to the forefront and the enemy would love for me to be pulled off course and distracted from becoming the woman of God that You destined and designed before the foundations of the world. Lord, I speak over myself and others for continued faith. I speak into the spirit for the days ahead where I may feel faint, lethargic or even spiritually empty.

God, I rest in YOU. You told me that I could dwell in YOUR secret place and that I can abide under YOUR shadow and You will fill me up to continue opposing the inappropriate forces. You told me that when I am weak, YOU will make me strong and I can mount up with eagle wings. It is during those times of opposition that I desire the wing span of an eagle and his ability to see. It is in those times when I need sustenance I realize that it can only come from YOU; for YOU know all things and you see the battles that I encounter and, more importantly, You know what's ahead of me.

I bind the spirit of fear and torment and speak peace into my life. I thank You for the increase of knowledge, wisdom and strength and the ability to stand upon YOU, YOUR WORD and upon the Rock, Christ Jesus. If I've neglected to mention or cover anything in the spirit regarding this particular area of my life, I speak now and ask You, Lord, for Your foreknowledge to keep me covered. Fill up those holes in the spirit, in Jesus' name I pray, amen and amen!

Day 24 – Stability

ear Lord, as I lay before You, I ask You to teach me about stability. Lord, oftentimes it is difficult to remain in a place of position because of those I might be connected to or even because of my own instability that might be based on my past experiences, hurts, pains and/or perceptions. Yet today, Lord, as I stand before Your throne in a spirit of humility and nakedness, I lay my problems at Your feet and on the altar.

You told me that if I take up my cross and follow You, I could be free. To do that, I am aware that I must first lay down my life. Thus Lord, here I am--Your broken vessel of honor. Lord take my life and rearrange and reshape it for I am clay that is on Your potter's wheel for a redesign that I might be redefined from this point forward in my purpose. From this point forward, Lord, I will stand before You as a whole and stable woman of God.

Even as the pressures come, I thank You NOW for the mind to stand in position as YOU see fit. Lord, MY STRENGTH comes from You daily. My wisdom comes from You daily. I know of no other way to live or survive through the seasons that are to come. You are my shelter, my Rock, my very mindset in regards to

Kingdom-building, for Lord I want to be able to reach out effectively to my husband, my family and those I am connected to in the area of stability.

Lord, teach me to be an example that I will not allow my emotions to rule my life. Lord, teach me discipline in regards to stability. Lord, any spiritual information that is downloaded in my spirit I realize it is manifested in Heaven and placed in my spirit and mind to be carried out here on earth.

Lord, it is ALL YOU! I worship You for who You are and, more so, who YOU are in MY life. I stand before You in a spirit of humility, thanking You for all You've done and what is to come in regards to my life in the area of stability.

I place worship in the atmosphere acknowledging You and Your right to either set me up or down for You know all things about me. I was made to accommodate Your love and worship, and, Lord, even if You slay me I WILL trust YOU. Lord, show favorable increase to me as You see fit. I oppose now, today, in the spirit any who come to maim, destroy or un-work the works of God's hand in this area in my life. I stand at heaven's doors and stand in position to be able to teach others what stability will do in their lives. Lord, it is never for my glory but always for You. Any spiritual construct that I have neglected to mention in my prayers this morning, Lord, I ask for Your covering and for Your mercy, in Jesus' name I pray, amen and amen!

Day 25 - Teaching of the Word

ear Lord, as I lay before You, I ask You to teach me about the clarity of Your Word and how it applies to my life in each situation and season I encounter. Lord, teach me about the purity of my heart, mind and spirit that I might speak into the life of my husband, my family and those to whom I am connected. Lord, in my quest for love and knowledge of You, I ask that You continue to give me guidance in this area, for I can never operate without You in my life. I can never move one step to the right, to the left, or forward without strength, understanding and knowledge from You.

Lord, I am YOUR servant and I desire to complete the tasks that have been set before me. It is with joy that I reach to obtain all that YOU have declared in this season of my life, knowing that it will propel me into the next level of my anointing. God, my desire is for YOU first, all else becomes secondary, for I am aware that seeking You first helps me reach the goals that are set before me.

Seeking You first strengthens me and teaches me to have an ongoing atmosphere of praise and worship that manifests occurrences of shifts in the spirit. Those shifts allow me to go in and pull down strongholds from satan; and so Lord, here I stand before You asking for everything I need to accomplish the journey.

Lord, for those who would stand with satan against me, I bind those forces now and in the future. For those who are not pure of heart, mind and spirit, I uncover them now for the future. Allow my spiritual sense, scent and vision to be increased. Allow me fortitude of strength to withstand any areas of lack in regards to the teaching of the Word. I ask that You grant me permission now to cover those areas in the spirit for my husband, my family and those to whom I am connected.

Lord, You fill the voids that are lacking for I cannot see all, but I do serve a God who can see, and I worship You for that. I praise Your precious name for YOU are Alpha and Omega, the Beginning and the End. I stand before You with humbleness of mind and spirit and thank You for what You have done and for what You are GOING to do.

Keep me Father and manifest all spiritual components as You see fit. Let no rift come between my husband and me. Let no strategy come between what You have stated in the spirit about us. Allow all things between us to be on one accord, in Jesus' name I pray, amen and amen!

Day 26 – Balance

*D*ear Lord, as I lay before You, I ask You to teach me about balance in my life. I need the ability to hear You specifically in this area because it is important to understand and be aware that my mainline of communication and growth is my ability to be connected to You, and balance is a key component of life.

Your Word states that "a double-minded man is unstable in all his ways." Lord, I have no desire to be double-minded. I choose to have ONE mind and need that mind to answer the call and direction of my design as the woman of God you created me to be. The enemy always desires to sift mankind as wheat, but as long as I am hearing from heaven I ask that You show me the attacks and the abnormalities in the spirit concerning any and all situations in my life, the life of my husband, my family and those to whom I am connected.

It is not just about a natural hearing but more so a spiritual tuning in to God Himself. Yes, the natural ear is my ability to process the information; but if the process of information is neither in tune nor in key with the Spirit of our Father, the understanding becomes null and void, and so I speak this into the atmosphere today. I ask for additional clarity surrounding balance, and if any person connects to me that is not of Your mindset, Lord allow me to not only hear with supernatural ability, but allow me to see their agenda and take appropriate steps to shut it down in the spirit.

I refuse to fight my spiritual battles with my flesh, but I step into the spirit to pull down all inappropriate strongholds. Lord I want to be on YOUR agenda and I refuse to submit to foolishness in my life or any and all contrary agendas of the enemy or any person that is his servant. Lord I am here for You, I am on Your agenda and I am for building up and assisting in YOUR Kingdom.

Continue to teach me about humility and servitude toward You. I ask for covering for any areas that are lacking balance in my life, my husband's life, my family and those to whom I am connected. Lord, show me the lack but more so teach me the wherewithal to straighten those areas and make my path straight and balanced. I bind all works of darkness in this area now and in the seasons to come.

God, You are preparing me for mighty works and I am grateful for Your presence in and around MY life. I speak peace, clarity, undeniable understanding and knowledge and declare that I shall go forth and conquer in YOUR name, the only name that stands, the only name that saves mankind from our sins and that name is Jesus. All this I ask for in faith believing it is MINE, in Jesus' name I pray, amen and amen!

Day 27 – Focus

ear Lord, as I lay before You, I ask You to teach me about the concept of focus in regards to my spiritual life, my husband, my family and those I am connected to as we continue on the path that God as set before us. Lord, let it be clear to me that I must remain focused on my destiny and not stop to socialize or "pick flowers" along the way, because those are the things that come to distract me from my true purpose.

There are those with whom I have connected in the past who did not have the ability to complete the tasks that God has asked of them. They can easily do things in the natural; and be successful at it, but working in God's Kingdom takes warriors trained to combat the enemy. So, Lord, I ask that You continue to give me clarity surrounding the seeds of focus; its concept and the understanding so that it might be produced in MY life, so I can minister to those who are hungry for it in their spirit. Lord, often they are not even aware of the hunger from the depths of their soul for distractions have been placed before them and those distractions have become their norm.

Lord, I am Your handmaiden and I speak understanding and foreknowledge in this particular area and bind up the works of darkness that come to steal, kill, destroy and deceive. Lord, I know that just as satan sends distractions and deception, YOU give clarity, understanding, knowledge but more so truth; and as I move forward, truth shall always be my guide. So I speak truth about focus, Lord, into my heart and mind. Where I lack, I ask that Your Holy Spirit sends a standard in that area for covering, and send a shaking in the spirit that I might rise to each occasion.

Lord, I ask that You close the gap immediately and expeditiously. In addition, I ask that You cover any area I neglected to mention. I speak peace and deliverance and ask that fruit follow my path and footsteps. I appreciate Your continued love in my life and worship You for who YOU are, a God of love, accountability and endurance, in spite of me. Thank You for continued deliverance, understanding and foreknowledge, in Jesus' name I pray, amen and amen!

Day 28 – Discernment

*D*ear Lord, as I lay before You, I ask You to teach me about the spirit of discernment. Lord, as I increase in this area I will be able to look back and see so many mistakes and missed areas, connections and seasons that I missed and was unaware of because of my lack of understanding and spiritual discernment, an ability You have bestowed upon Your people.

Lord, I want to be able to see with "YOUR EYES," for me, my husband, my family and those to whom I am connected. So, Lord, I will maintain position as I continue to grow in this area and become aware that my relationship with You can never become stagnant, for that would mean I am not striving, growing or pressing toward the mark. As long as I live on this earth, I must press until You come because situations and people are rarely true to form.

Things might continually come to disappoint me, but I stand on a solid rock, Christ Jesus, and my relationship with You ALWAYS make things worthwhile. So, Lord, I place in the atmosphere today a desire for increase in the area of discernment. As I move forward and the seasons shift, change, increase and begin to unfold, I ask You Lord to give clarity and understanding to cut through any situation. Discerning is my ability to know, but discerning is also a gift from You, and it would appear in these end times that many are using it for their own agenda and not for Kingdom-building.

God, as Your humble servant, I stand before You asking You to cover me, my husband, my family and those to whom I am connected. Keep us humble and pliable to You and before YOU. Never allow our ability to know to be in conflict with YOUR will and YOUR way. We realize we must always be in alignment with YOU to minister to others.

Lord, send increased knowledge to us. Download into our spirits the methods YOU want us to move forward in to make the best use of others' abilities and gifts. I place that in the atmosphere to ripen the ground, so when seeds of knowledge drop it will fall on good ground to be nurtured to reap a full harvest. I speak against any area of disbelief, and request that it dissipate immediately.

Lord, unstop my spiritual ears for I realize that satan is the authority in this world's system, but YOU came to dispel all confusion and strife. I speak now (prophetically) for times to come. Anyone that comes to attack, maim or misalign my relationship, I stop them now in the spirit. I stand at hell's doors to take back to God what is rightfully His! God, I stand in position for others in the spirit. Give me the wherewithal to not only fight but conquer in the spirit. Lord, I stand and bind the works of the enemy by the power and authority given to me by the blood of the Lamb, Christ Jesus.

Lord, increase the sight of both my eyes in You. Give me clarity in all situations. In addition, send the type of clarity and intensity that can only come from You. Increase my desire for You. Increase my relationship with You. Make Your voice so articulate that I clearly know You have spoken. Make my ears and spirit so sensitive that the download is immediate and the path is made clear on the download. Any area I have neglected to mention surrounding the area of discernment I ask for Your covering in the spirit.

Plug any inappropriate holes and situations. I bind every evil work and any people or situations that don't line up with You, not only now but also in the future. I worship YOU and thank You for what You have done and what You are going to do in this particular area. Lord I thank YOU for YOUR discernment, in Jesus' name, amen and amen, and it is declared so!

Day 29 - Discipline

*D*ear Lord, as I lay before You, I ask You to teach me about discipline and the areas that need to be discerned concerning the upcoming season in my life, the life of my husband, my family and those to whom I am connected. God we speak increase into the atmosphere even now; increase in discipline, increase in understanding, increase in ability to give to others what You are speaking into my life.

My life does not belong to me, but, Lord, it belongs to You, and it is ALWAYS about service. I am called to serve others in the line of fire, and through this process, I have learned to do it with joy. For it is a joy to serve You first and foremost. Thus Lord, I begin to dig into the depths of the spirit and as in the Old Testament when the wells went dry, I begin to dig another well because I have YOUR favor.

What others cannot obtain or cannot spiritually see, I know does not apply to me because You have continually spoken over my life through worship, prophetic words, understanding, and knowledge.

Even now at this precise moment, Lord, I release clarity and precision into the atmosphere concerning discipline in every area of my life, for Lord, all this comes to naught if discipline is not intertwined throughout this process. Thus, I slice through every area that is NOT like You in the spirit, and at this moment, I pull down every stronghold that I personally might not feel can be attained and ask that You continue to give me YOUR eyes. For Lord, I can never fully see with my human eyes but I need YOUR eyes to see into the spirit.

Place plans of action in place to accommodate all that You have spoken and given by YOUR Word. Lord, I never want to rise above what YOU have said, but I always want to continue to abase myself. Cloak me with a spirit of humility that is seasoned with grace. Even so right now, Lord, I bind every wicked force that tries to compel thoughts from the enemy. I bind every wicked force that attempts for me and my husband to rise above the abasement of the Word of God and His essence of humility in our lives. Any unauthorized open doors I shut in the spirit at this precise moment. Continue to allow us to be aware of any opening that tries to encroach upon the territory that You have declared in both of our lives.

I speak to the spirits of fear, pain, recessed memories, inappropriate gestures of the enemy and bind it all and pull it down and cast it out in the name of the Lord Jesus! Even the high territorial spirits like Jezebel or any gatekeepers who seek to administer fear and pain through open doors of hurt, I speak against those, too. Lord, we leave no unauthorized open door as You continue to move us forward in the area of discipline.

Lord, if there are any around us who have contrary agendas to YOUR will, I bind the spirits that reside within them and declare that their control and agendas be bound and their permission to operate within our atmosphere has been revoked. Lord, You have spoken before about agenda-minded folk in my life and, thus, I ask for increased discernment to see them. Lord, put the boundaries of Your will in place and allow me to love but not be fooled; and show any anti-Christ spirit(s) forth immediately in the spirit, and allow them to fall by the wayside with no upsetting or drama in the atmosphere surrounding me, my husband, my family and those to whom I am connected.

The people who carry these spirits might not understand, but Lord, I do, for my battles are never with people but with the spiritual components of the enemy. I speak all these things into the atmosphere and thank You for continued knowledge, in Jesus' name I pray, amen and amen!

Day 30 – Praise and Worship

*D*ear Lord, as I lay before You, I ask You to teach me how praise and worship clears my atmosphere to propel me forward in my destiny. It also propels me forward in my relationships, marriage, and those to whom I am connected.

Lord, I am beginning to understand that worship is an intricate process that allows one to gain additional healing, for it is tied up in Your character and love. Worship speaks to the fact that none of us are ever worthy to approach You, but through Your Son, we have the ability to do something that places our worship above the angels.

Thus, Lord, I ask for additional clarity regarding praise and worship. Lord, often things You request of my life do not make clear sense initially, but I am trusting You. "Though You slay me, I will trust You." Though You allow me to go through many changes, I will trust You. I know that often when YOU articulate something to me, I don't always have immediate access to the thought process and often my understanding is murky at best. But this I do know: as I stand in faith and walk out the process all things will be made known.

Teach me to clearly WORSHIP YOU in spirit and in truth, so that understanding might be shared with others. This I do know also: that whenever Your Word is given, it is never given to me to hoard it for my personal enrichment, but it is given to impart to others as Your servant. I hear You, God! You are giving expanded knowledge and increase even right now.

All the spiritual components are being laid as a foundation of understanding; each concept is building in context and content to create a vast knowledgeable expansion of You. All things and all roads lead back to You. I am nothing without You. Even when I don't understand, I still acknowledge and worship You as the Creator and the One who is right and just, and has YOUR hand in my life.

I humbly submit to the process that You have laid out for me. You are the God of Glory and YOU show Your handiwork daily. Lord, You are teaching me that there is always a time frame and season in my life. Lord, teach me never to miss the seasons and windows of opportunity You have placed before me.

Satan would often have me miss out and keep me in a vicious cycle, a downward spiral of misunderstanding. But Lord, I break every wicked force right now and speak clarity into my thought process and my mind.

Teach me, Lord to admit my wrong as I humble myself before You in worship and acknowledgement. For, Lord, I know that approaching You always gains my healing; and I know it is for You to expend justice to those who have wronged me. Vengeance belongs to You and is never at my own hand.

Lord, I humbly submit to Your entire authority on my life and lay before Your presence to bask in Your healing powers. There is none like You, neither in the heavens nor in the earth. There is none to worship as such and You alone are God, for none can be compared to You. Your presence in my life is worth every struggle that I have encountered.

Just to have a glimpse of Your face is worth any hardship. Just as Moses asked to see Your face, Lord, show me Your face. Allow me to see Your hind-parts. Show me my past, present and future as I worship. Teach me to whisper intimate words of pure worship in Your ear and allow me to remain close to You as I rest in Your arms of grace.

Lord, there is none like You and this is why I worship--to understand, if only for a brief moment my pain and my issues. Lord, as the season changes, I ask that You give me all that I need to fulfill the call on my life. Lord, teach me how to approach Your throne for access to the balance of understanding in regards to my life. Lord, I place it in the atmosphere even so right now at THIS moment!

Give clarity, understanding of precision and access to what others struggle to find and see. I speak over myself a spirit of discernment and peace right now. I speak to the spirits that come to torment me and I bind every wicked force from the enemy. God, I understand that the enemy will try to thwart the works of You, but I bind him at this moment--all things will become clear and I WILL UNDERSTAND as I worship.

Worship slices through the spirits of torment and increases the enemy's confusion, thus, Lord, I bind the spirits of confusion around me, my husband, my family and those to whom I am connected. Lord, allow our worship to place a hedge of protection around us to gain additional strategy (strategies) for spiritual components, to propel us into our destiny. All this we ask in Jesus' name, amen, and it is so!

Day 31 – Love Motivates and Heals

*D*ear Lord, as I lay before You I ask You to teach me true and unconditional love. More so, Lord, give me clarity surrounding the expression of love that motivates and heals. Lord, as I lay before Your presence, this morning, it is with understanding that the love You have shown me allows me to transform that into unconditional love for my husband, my family and those to whom I am connected.

Often, my eyes get cloudy because of the hurt that is associated with loving others. But, God, You said that YOUR Word would never return unto You void; that whatever we give to others, You shall return. God, You know that my life journey as a woman often brings me sorrow but along with sorrow comes joy that YOU place in my spirit, and Lord I feel YOUR joy this morning as I bask in YOUR presence.

God, You have bestowed upon me a gift; and that gift is unconditional love, and Lord as I lay in worship and pray through each and every situation in my life, I ask that You increase the love for others in my heart. Lord, I want to be able to heal others with Your love. You told me in Your Word that Peter healed with his shadow. Lord, I am making this request of You today, I want my shadow to heal others, and as I walk by folk I want them to feel YOUR presence. I want them to see more of YOU than of me!

Let Your presence be made known, even when they don't understand. I declare that when I walk into a place, the atmosphere changes. Lord, from this day forward, nothing from the past will penetrate my life today. I request a complete shift in the spirit that will portray itself in the natural.

Lord, each time YOU showed up with a prophetic word it was true, precise and accurate. I believe today is no different because of my faith. Lord, even now, I stand in position to believe for myself and my husband, my family and those to whom I am connected.

God, how can I even express my love for You? There are no words, but my spirit cries out, "Abba Father," and, "Lord, I love You." Lord, please allow my crown to become complete in this season. Forever, Lord, I will worship Your Glory.

Lord, as I continue the path You have designated for my life, I ask that You allow the love that You have shown toward me to become apparent to all those around me, and that You allow me to love others enough to heal their minds, their spirits but most of all, their souls, for it is not ME doing the healing but You alone God.

Lord, I speak against any and every contrary spirit that fights against the dominion of the Almighty in my life. I demand that you return to the pit of hell immediately. God has spoken release in my life, and so be it by the precious blood of the Lamb, the power and authority is in the name and blood of Jesus Christ. Lord, thank YOU for all that You have done and what YOU will continue to do in YOUR name. I bow before You in reverence of Your power, authority and glory, amen and amen!

And, as it is written, so be it from this point forward. My continual journey of pouring out and loving has been completed by God's authority and will in MY life.

The Proverbs 31 Woman
A Modern Day Perspective

A wise woman builds her house (Proverbs 14:1), means she builds her house with the labor of her love. She does not purposely destroy, nor does she allow another access, which also means she builds her man up with encouragement and love with an intensity that translates to the man who realizes the treasure he has found. If he is not treasuring you, ask yourself what you are doing wrong.

Proverbs 27:15 teaches us that it is not healthy for a woman to neither fuss nor be quarrelsome. Do you feel the need to have the last word or you always have to be right? Remember, you are not the head, but were made/equipped to assist/stand at his side, but if you continually destroy your house you will have nothing left.

If the heart is the wellspring of life (Proverbs 4:23), then the mind could be the channel that determines the process of the outcome, meaning one must decide what level of relationship that one lets into his or her life/heart. One must guard through their thought process and then choose wisely. Best way to play that game is through your relationship with God/prayer. GAME ON.

Before you give anyone advice, ask God what you should say. This might alleviate some problems you might cause others by trying to be a counselor without consulting God. (Proverbs 11:14/15:22)

Proverbs 31:1-31

A mother can influence her children, and her love is powerful. It teaches, it heals, it uplifts and has the ability to place vision in the heart of a child.

Proverbs 31:1-2

Mothers, teach your young men not to give their strength or heart to a woman ahead of time, teach them stay away from things that destroy, teach them to look for the inward components of a woman, her strength and her wisdom. Teach them to look for her ability to be able to love, support and uplift.

Proverbs 31:3

Mothers, teach your young men not to be inebriated (drunk), for then they cannot rule properly, they afflict others, forget what they are supposed to do and cause havoc; but teach them that they should look after those who are down in spirit and need assistance.

Proverbs 31:4-7

Men have the ability to speak for others and keep them from paths of destruction. They are judgers of what is good and what is right, they do know how to uplift those who are oppressed and in spiritual straights.

Proverbs 31:8-9

A wife is worth more than jewels. She is precious. She must be sought out to find. Her character is above reproach. Once found, you must continue to seek after her heart and she will keep you safe, more importantly you can find rest in her.

Proverbs 31:10-12

Can you be trusted in your relationship? Are the intimate details of your husband kept safely within your heart/mind/spirit? Or are you one of those women who will put him on 'blast?' Learn to keep his heart hidden within yours.

Proverbs 31:11

Ladies, are you busy taking care of home? Or are you busy meddling, hanging with your girls, talking about everybody 'round the way, down the block?' Be about your man's business first.

Proverbs 31:13-15

To get a handle in your relationship, it makes sense to seek the Master Designer about the man in your life. A consistent prayer life works wonders. Prayer before the day begins often alleviates disasters throughout the day. Provide for your family through prayer. Family first--ALWAYS!

Proverbs 31:15

Ladies, we are powerful when we minister to each other. Yet so often we are selfish and hoard; this denotes a certain lack of freedom on our part. Learn to share and free up some negative spiritual space, and give to those who are not as fortunate as you.

Proverbs 31:15-17

Ladies, put your money to good use, think of others, or family. Focus on your future. You are strong in spirit and mentally able to accomplish much more, however, you must stay busy with purpose, for in your womb you are capable of birthing destiny to yourself and others.

Proverbs 31:18-19

Ladies, share your wealth in terms of knowledge, spirit and love.

Proverbs 31:20

Ladies, prepare your household for stormy weather. Do not be caught off guard in spirit or in terms of the heart. Be the Queen that God called you to be.

Proverbs 31:21-22

Ladies, did you know that your husband is known by the works that you do? The wealth that you obtain and share in knowledge and in spirit means he can sit among his boys knowing all is well; and his woman has his best interests at heart.

Proverbs 31:23

Dignified ladies can strut their stuff. They are strong, wise, full of strength, knowledge and grace. Everybody knows her value and who she is, what she does, and what is given to others at the Master's request. She is in tune to His Voice.

Proverbs 31:24-25

Ladies be wise, kind and instruct in love.

Proverbs 31:26

Ladies, you can't be all up in somebody else's biz and expect for home to stay together. Let's keep it real. Home is first. Family is first--ALWAYS!

Proverbs 31:27

Ladies, your children will grow up and acknowledge the virtues of you; for a well-kept home-life allows your children and your husband to look to you with praise, knowing their well-being is kept hidden deep in your heart and spirit.

Proverbs 31:28

Ladies, daughters of the King excel in all that they do. THEY ARE QUEENS! THEY STAND ABOVE ALL THE REST!

Proverbs 31:29

So many believe that beauty is an outward component, when in reality beauty lies within one's heart; it never fades, is graceful, is elegant, never deceptive, and always looks for direction from above.

Proverbs 31:30

Queen's daughters willingly give of themselves, are transparent, and all who meet them know this, they are known by their works, not by their mouth.

Proverbs 31:31

Seek to know that you might grow.

Belinda

Biography

Belinda Esther Oliver, or as she is affectionately called "Bee" or "Queen Bee," is a visionary administrator, who is often asked to sit on community boards to share a fresh perspective on daily administrative problems.

She is the president of Jireh's Promise, a non-profit organization focused on community responsibility, economic and community development, holistic health care and preventive services. Jireh's Promise incorporates a spiritual component to a humanistic curriculum, demonstrating the compassion of Christ through service to local communities. Belinda has a vision to take this grass-roots concept throughout the United States.

Belinda is a fourth-generation, "preacher's kid," who grew up using her talents in many areas of ministry. She has held positions as an altar worker, Sunday School teacher, worship leader, choir member, secretary, chief-of staff/assistant to state presidents', van driver, computer technician, and newsletter editor. Last, but definitely not least, Bee is a Worshiper and equates her relationship with God to breathing; she would cease to exist without His presence in her life.

Belinda's ability to see visionary components in the lives of others allows her to share information to assist in a life change. She loves to help people and realizes 'assisting' is her passion. Belinda has mentored and counseled many over the years and is ecstatic when one who she has assisted comes back to share good news.

Belinda believes in healthy marriages and often you might find her having a conversation with some of the men in helping them to understand their wives. Her goal is to make sure they are aware that they have a responsibility to love their wives as Christ loves His people. On the other hand, she instructs wives to unselfishly love their husbands and that submission truly holds power. It is quite clear that her coaching is never gender-biased. Belinda is quite aware that freedom often begins in the mind first and that the cognitive thought process plays a significant role in societal struggles. She is in the process of completing her B.S. in Psychology to further increase her skill and understanding.

Belinda has many books forthcoming that deal with practical daily living and healthy relationships. She uses, "Teaching Lessons...Defining Moments," as a tool to give readers insight into, and clarity about, various situations in their lives from a Godly perspective. It is with understanding that each test and trial she now goes through is another "chapter" for one of her various books. Belinda says, "The only limitations you will encounter are the ones you put on yourself." She firmly believes one must make an effort to change and be an active participant in the process. Belinda is all about change for herself and her community.

Belinda stands in the role of a mother and supporter to three young men, Scott, a culinary chef and recent graduate of Johnson & Wales University; Joshua and Josiah.

Belinda is a contributor to online magazines, websites and local newspapers.

You can contact Belinda at:

http://belindaeoliver.com

https://twitter.com/belindaeoliver

https://www.facebook.com/belindaeoliver2

http://www.linkedin.com/in/belindaeoliver

CPSIA information can be obtained at www.ICGtesting.com
Printed in the USA
BVOW010037150113

310554BV00002B/71/P